PIANO SOLO

THE BOOK THIEF

MUSIC FROM THE MOTION PICTURE SOUNDTRACK
COMPOSED AND ARRANGED FOR PIANO BY JOHN WILLIAMS

ISBN 978-1-4803-7062-3

HAL•LEONARD®
CORPORATION

7777 W. BLUEMOUND RD. P.O. BOX 13819 MILWAUKEE, WI 53213

In Australia Contact:
Hal Leonard Australia Pty. Ltd.
4 Lentara Court
Cheltenham, Victoria, 3192 Australia
Email: ausadmin@halleonard.com.au

Visit Hal Leonard Online at
www.halleonard.com

THE VISITOR

Composed by JOHN WILLIAMS

Reflectively "With Nostalgia"

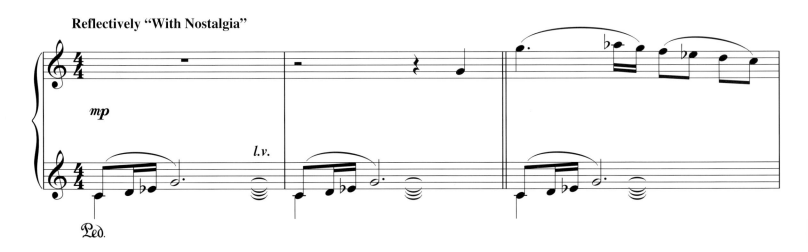

THE BOOK THIEF

Composed by JOHN WILLIAMS

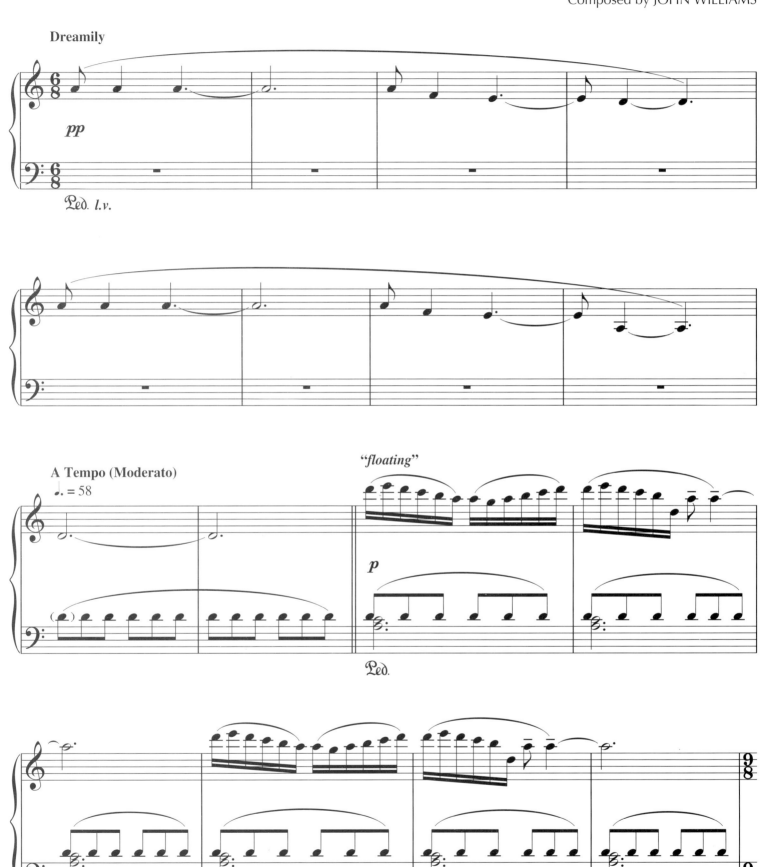

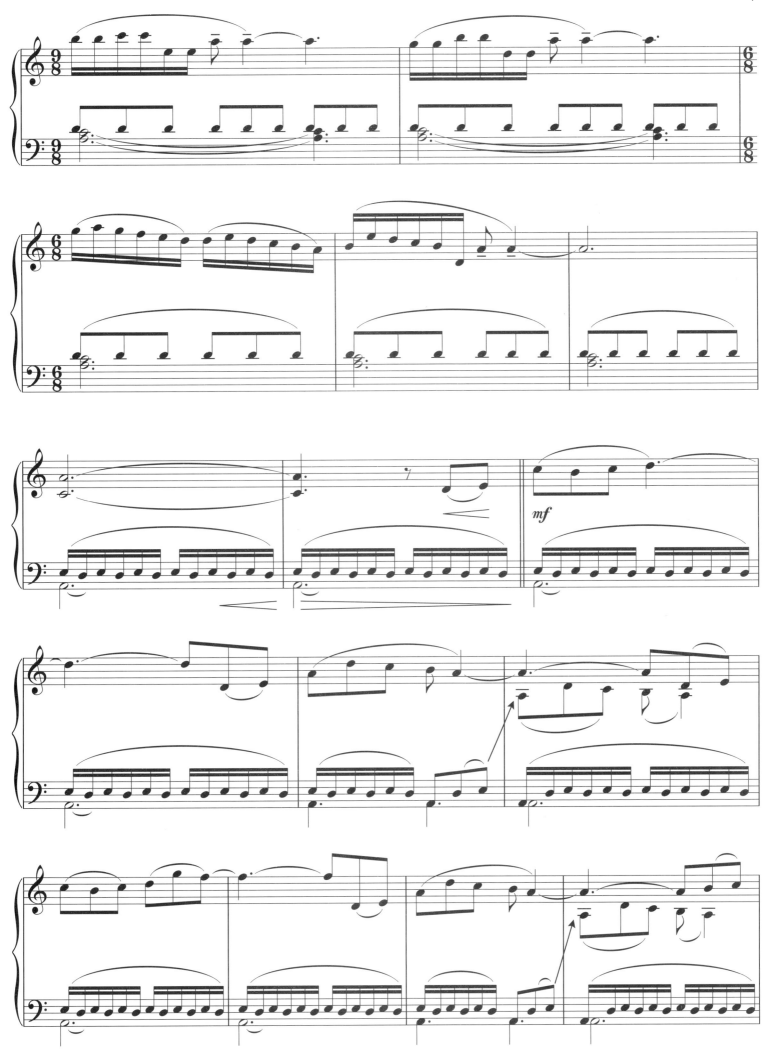

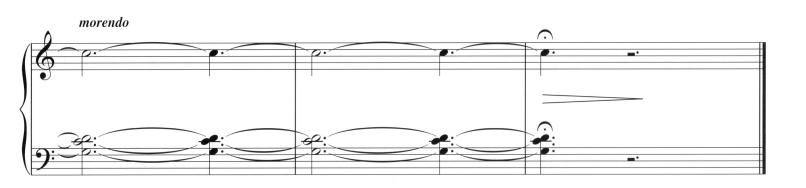

THE SNOW FIGHT

Composed by JOHN WILLIAMS

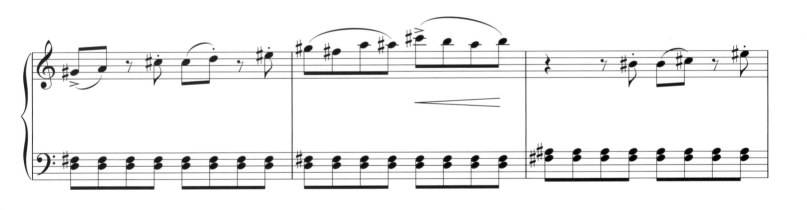

12

Tempo 1º (Subito) ♩ = 80

MAX AND LIESEL

Composed by JOHN WILLIAMS

Reflectively

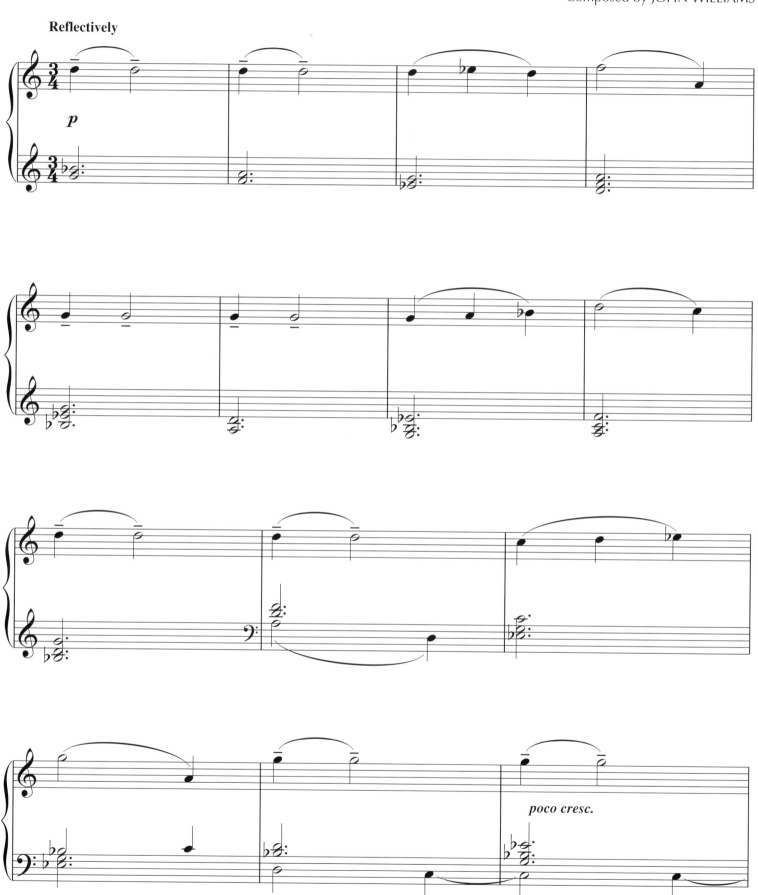

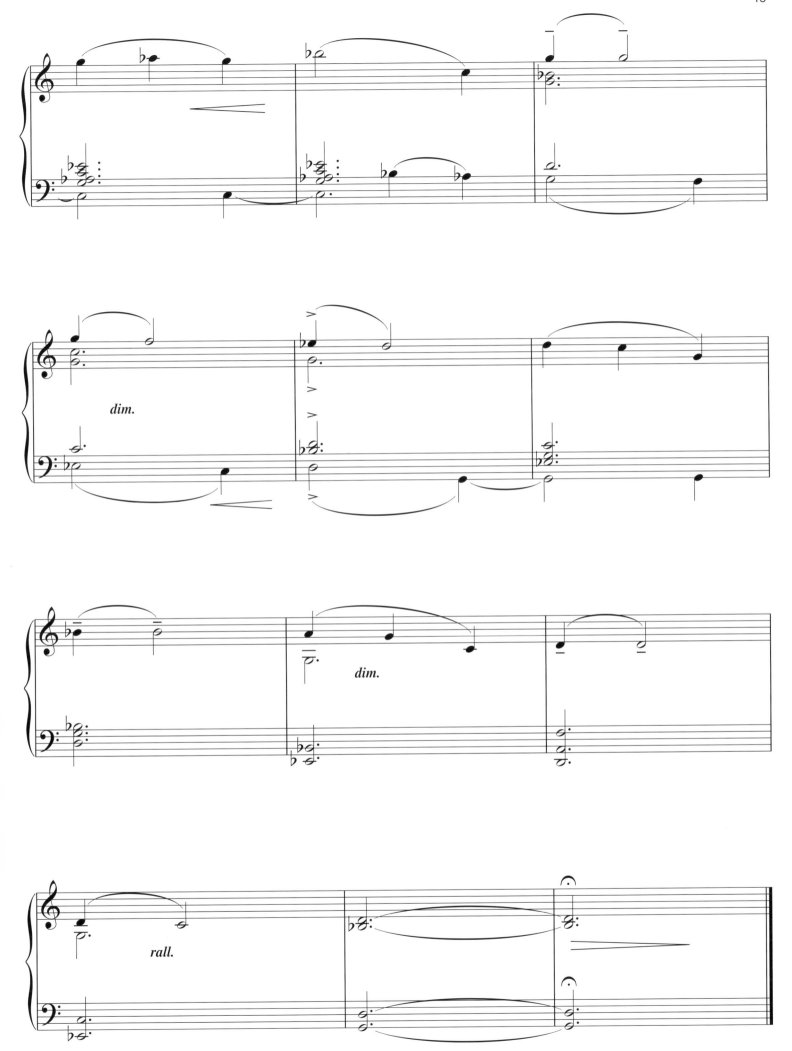

THE VISITOR AT HIMMEL STREET

Composed by JOHN WILLIAMS

Andante ♩. = 48

LEARNING TO READ

Composed by JOHN WILLIAMS

Take Time

Flowing again ♩ = 60

MAX'S DEPARTURE

Composed by JOHN WILLIAMS